A Scottish Childhood

Growing up a Baby Boomer

Ann Burnett

Published by Ladybug Publications

ISBN 978 0 9558540 9 5

To my family members and friends, past and present, who have contributed, intentionally or otherwise, to this book.
Thanks for the memories.

Contents

Introduction

I wrote a series of articles for the magazine *Scottish Memories* from 2013 until its demise in 2017. The articles were all about growing up in the West of Scotland after the Second World War and were illustrated by my father's photographs that he took of us.

Bill Ferguson was a keen amateur photographer, winning prizes in newspapers and magazines, and he did his own enlarging and developing in a workshop attached to the large old house he'd rented for us all in Glasgow. When he married my mother in 1941, he also took on her mother and any of her four brothers when they came home on leave

from fighting in the war. He, being a chemist specialising in lubricants, was deemed essential to the war effort and excluded from serving in the armed forces.

Bill took numerous photos of us as children going about the business of growing up and we became either quite immune to his requests to look at the camera and pose or gloriously hammed it up in front of the lens.

Through the haze of nostalgia, it seems an idyllic childhood but there was trouble on the horizon. When we were still quite young, the marriage broke up, not a common occurrence in the 50s among ordinary working class folk, and he left the family home.

We eventually were forced to leave too as we could no longer afford the upkeep of the house.

The photographs became few and far between then. But for those few years when we were ostensibly a happy family, and his camera was always in his hand, his photographs have left a unique legacy of our childhood which I only now can appreciate.

This book gathers those articles together with the addition of further photos from his collection.

Growing up After the Second World War

I'm a baby boomer, born just after the end of the Second World War when the men were returning home. Not only did I receive a birth certificate to recognise my arrival, I

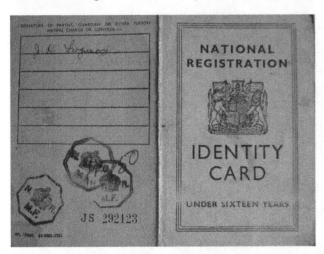

was also given a National Registration Identity Card when I was nine days old. I had no idea I had this document until I was clearing out my mother's things after her death. I certainly never remember using it.

Like all babies born at this time, my clothes were all hand-knitted or sewn, borrowed or handed down. Nappies were terry towelling and, as there were no plastic pants then, left damp patches everywhere. The pram, cot, nursing chair and other equipment were all acquired from others whose children had grown. In fact, when my brother arrived a couple of years later, things were no better and he slept in the bottom drawer of a chest of drawers.

Food was still rationed though babies were supplied with dried milk and eggs, concentrated orange juice, cod liver oil and rose hip syrup to build us up. The 'green

ladies' (health visitors in heavy green serge coats) came regularly to check on our progress and to offer advice to mothers.

But there were a lot of us around and the crux came when we started school. Over 50 children, including myself, arrived at Angus Oval Primary School to go into the infants class. The room wasn't big enough, there weren't enough seats and they were short of teachers so it was decided that

we would come in two lots, half in the morning and half in the afternoon. Part-time education in other words. That suited me fine. I wasn't keen on school. The teacher, Mrs Ferguson, had two small children of her own and had been brought back into teaching to help solve the teacher shortage.The fact that she was an old school-friend of my mother did not endear me any more to the educational system. I howled that first day.

Mrs Ferguson and her P1 class. I'm in the back row, second pupil on the left.

We were each given a slate, a piece of chalk and a mini sized blackboard duster. On our slate we were expected to copy the letters on the blackboard that Mrs Ferguson had put up. Each was done in the shape of an item beginning with that letter, *a* was an apple, *b* a bat and ball, *c* a cat….. The one I remember best was *f*, done as a beautiful purple and pink feather. There was a little story for each letter which the class would chant in unison and *f*'s was '*Fanny's funny feather says fii'*. That's the only one I can remember .

The same reading book was given to every child and was to last the whole year. Each week we learned a new page and again chanted along with the teacher. As I had read the whole book on the first night I got it home, I found this incredibly boring. It was all I could do to keep the place on the page while we each read a sentence round the class.

Many years later, when both my mother and Mrs Ferguson were in their nineties, the teacher paid a visit to her old friend. I took her coat and led her into the lounge. She fixed me with her teacher's gimlet eye and said, 'You were a right wee b.....r in school!' I suppose she was right!

Grandma Jane – My Personal Outfitter

After the war, my Grandma Jane's skills as a tailoress were much in demand. As she lived with us, I was the frequent beneficiary of her sewing and knitting talents.

When Grandma wanted to sew, a fire was lit in the grate in the spare bedroom where her Singer treadle sewing machine was set up. She would sit there for hours treadling away at coats, suits, dresses as well as household items like turning sheets end to end. As it was usually the warmest room, I would join her and play with my dolls at her feet. The rhythmic sound of the treadle was an accompaniment to my childhood.

My brother and I must have been the best-dressed kids on the block. Take the matching red trousers, coats and hats trimmed with black velvet that she made for us. And notice the large turn-ups on the trousers; no, not for fashion but for our growth! Every item of clothing she made for us had room for our growth in the shape of huge hems on dresses and skirts, sleeves which could be lengthened and for anything that fastened at the shoulder, she made extra long straps so the buttons could be moved. However, I didn't like everything Grandma Jane made for me. A brown fur coat and hat made me look like a teddy bear and was rather heavy on my thin shoulders. Its weight increased greatly if it happened to rain while I was wearing it as the fur fabric absorbed water like a sponge.

Grandma loved making my summer dresses, though they never had the circular skirt I yearned for. They all came with matching knickers which had a pocket in them for my hankie. I never, ever kept a hankie there. I was not for hoicking up my skirt every time I wanted to blow my nose. She was also a beautiful knitter, turning out jumpers and cardigans, clothes for my dolls and intricate Argyle patterned socks. She kept the various wools wound on to what we called 'doo hickeys' to stop them becoming entangled with each other.

She even knitted swimsuits for my brother and I for our annual holidays 'doon the watter' in Millport or Arran. Mine was dark green and Alan's was dark blue, but they were not a success as when wet and water-logged, they stretched down to our knees, leaving our skinny chests bare.

Grandma Jane's piece de resistance was my ballet dress. Masses of white net for the skirt and a white satin bodice with a matching satin head-band. I loved it and was so proud to wear it at my ballet school's annual show. There was nothing she wouldn't turn her hand to. Her embroidery decorated tablecloths, cushions, lavender bags to hand out as Christmas presents,

dressing table sets (remember them?) handkerchiefs, even milk jug covers, the edges beaded to weigh them down. Each and every one was beautifully made. She taught me (very patiently) to sew and knit but I didn't have anything like her talent for it, or her magic touch, so I must have been a bit of a disappointment to her.

Nothing ever went to waste. She made bed covers out of the scraps of material left

over from her dress-making. She would sew strips and odd squares together until the piece was big enough, fold it in half and inside, sew in an old worn blanket to give it extra bulk and warmth. I still have one of them, and seeing it brings back memories. It's a bit faded and crumpled now but still usable if not exactly pretty.

Measles and Mumps

Every spring without fail, my younger brother would contract one of the many childhood illnesses that abounded in the 50s and 60s, and equally without fail, he would pass it on to me. So, just as he was recovering, I would succumb. Measles, chicken pox, whooping cough, mumps and many other unidentifiable ailments we shared between us. Because we were considered infectious, we were kept in isolation from

other children until the danger had passed.

I didn't mind too much. After a few days of feeling pretty miserable, I was usually well enough to enjoy my cosy bed surrounded by my books, jigsaws, box of treasures and dolls. The fire would have been lit in the bedroom, there would be a hot drink by my bed and best of all, I didn't have to go to school. Yes, the spots were itchy though soothed with pink calamine lotion, yes I didn't feel like eating much though one of Granny's sweeties could always tempt me, and no, I wasn't missing school one bit.

Measles however, did have lasting consequences. After Jackie had it, she had to wear glasses ever after. 'It weakened my eyes,' she says. 'When I was ill, I couldn't bear the light and I was kept in a darkened room. I didn't even feel well enough to celebrate Christmas so it was postponed till I was better.'

Whooping cough was also nasty. My brother took it when just four months old and was very ill. Of course, I took it after him and my poor exhausted mother thought a holiday at the seaside with all that fresh sea air would build us up. Unfortunately it

September holiday in Millport. I'm clutching a tin of dried milk.

turned out to be a typical West of Scotland September – wet, windy and cold.

Dave, one of five children, remembers when they all caught chicken pox at the same time. 'Mum made a "ward" for us in the living room where we were ensconced on armchairs and the settee. It supposedly made it easier for her and meant we could entertain each other once we were feeling better.'

But the scourge of the 1950s was polio. Until polio vaccinations were introduced in 1955, every summer brought the fear of an epidemic. Swimming pools were believed to be a source of the infection so children were kept away from them. I remember two children in my primary school who had contracted the infection and had lost the use of their legs. They had to use heavy metal and leather callipers thereafter.

So great was the anxiety that polio engendered that when Margaret's parents discovered that her brother was having difficulty walking, they immediately sent for the doctor. It was only when he was undressed that they discovered that he had both legs down one leg of his underpants!

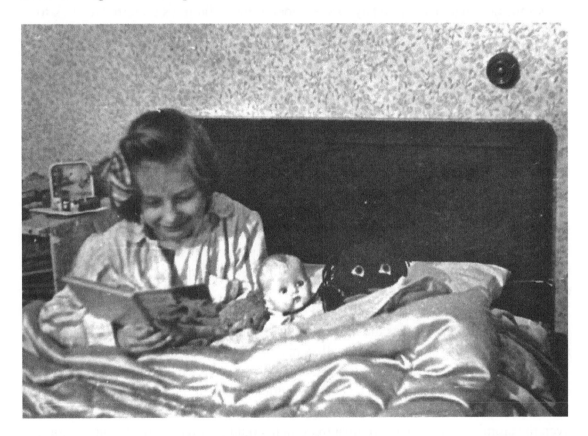

In an attempt to bolster the health of the 'baby boomers', those children born after the Second World War when the men were returning home, the new National Health Service provided free orange juice for all youngsters. I remember the bottles filled with the thick, bright yellow liquid which was diluted with water. Delicious! Not such a favourite was the free cod liver oil which came in similar bottles and was dispensed in daily tablespoonfuls, usually with a drink of the orange juice after to get rid of the taste.

And who can forget Virol, that sweet, sticky, treacle-like substance that was guaranteed to build up poorly children? It came in big brown jars with a wide mouth

11

large enough for a good sized tablespoon. Sandra was lucky, her dad worked at Johnnie Walkers and brought home jars of the stuff, malt extract being used in the whisky industry.

For vitamin C, when fruit and veg were scarce over the winter months, there was rose hip syrup, a delicate pink liquid, a teaspoonful of which went down a treat.

Being 'regular' was a matter of great concern in most households and castor oil was the solution. However, my mother remembered it only too well from her own childhood so we were fortunate enough never to get it, relying instead on California Syrup of Figs to sort any problems.

Despite no longer having to pay to see a doctor, many families preferred to stick to old and trusted home remedies. Do you remember the second verse of the old nursery rhyme, *Jack and Jill*?

Up Jack got and home did trot
As fast as he could caper,
He went to bed to mend his head
With vinegar and brown paper.

Vinegar was still used in the 1950's for soothing bee stings and sore throats. Jim remembers gargling with a teaspoon of vinegar in warm water and being careful not to swallow it as he didn't like the taste.

What the healing properties of brown paper were, I can't imagine but brown paper was frequently mentioned as a remedy for chest infections like bronchitis. Dave recalls his mother liberally rubbing Vick on his chest, wrapping brown paper round him, putting on his liberty bodice and sending him off to school where, every time he moved at his desk, he rustled.

Vick was frequently used for colds and coughs, as were poultices made out of all sorts of materials. Kaolin was the most popular but there were also mustard, sugar and soap, raw potato and bread poultices, all slapped on as hot as was bearable.

One solution for constant colds and infections was to have the tonsils removed. Not a pleasant experience for many. Dave and Sandra both recall the sight of that horrible black mask descending, the smell of the gas and being sick after it was all over. Not even the promise of ice-cream, a great treat then, could mollify them. Hospitals didn't allow mothers to stay with their children then so there were many very upset children in the wards. However, Jim's tonsils were removed on his granny's kitchen table, scrubbed specially for the event. Granny had neglected to let his mother know this was happening and there were strong words afterwards.

Alcohol was a popular cure-all in households where drink was acceptable and not regarded as an evil. Hot toddies of whisky, water and honey or sugar helped soothe sore throats and toothache while a teaspoon of brandy or gin and water helped settle a sore tummy. More than likely, the alcohol knocked us out to sleep. Margaret, recovering from a nasty stomach upset and getting ready for bed, was never allowed to forget her reminding her mother to bring up the gin!

I remember butter balls for sore throats, lumps of butter rolled in sugar which you sucked. They always seemed to work. Lavender water splashed on one of my granny's clean hankies and placed on my forehead was a remedy for headache. Perhaps it did have aromatherapy properties.

Nowadays, with the prevalence of antibiotics children are quick to recover from any illnesses and vaccination programmes have all but eradicated many childhood diseases. But in the 1950s and before, an illness was regarded as much more serious and treated accordingly. We were 'cootered', closely watched and looked after, and I for one, didn't mind that at all.

My First Public Performance

Being such a shy wee girl and very clingy, my mother decided to encourage me to branch out and be more sociable so she enrolled me in an infant's dance class in Mosspark, Glasgow. This class was for pre-school children and was run by a Miss McLeod, who also took ballet and highland dance classes. The classes were held in a

My parents liked to dance... and so did we!

small hall just off Paisley Road West which was obviously used for adult dancing as well as there was a notice pinned to the wall inside which read, 'No BeBopping Allowed.' I hadn't a clue what that meant but it sounded fascinating.

Each year in May, the Hopkins School of Dancing, of which Miss McLeod was a part, held an annual ball where the students demonstrated their prowess in all the various forms of dancing that they had been taught. And the infants were to be part of it! For some reason, I had been chosen to lead the rest of my class in our Pillow Dance, which consisted of holding a small pram pillow and parading slowly around turning this way and that, until at the end we held the pillows to our cheeks and pretended to fall asleep.

The great day arrived. The ball was to be held in the McLellan Galleries on Sauchiehall Street on a Saturday afternoon so that all the mums and dads and grannies could attend. I was dressed in my party dress and my pillow had a fresh embroidered pillow slip put on it 'so as not to show us up' as my mother put it. The audience sat on three sides around the dance floor. My little class was seated right in the front row so we could see the other dancers' performances. Unfortunately, when I turned round, I could see my mother sitting just a couple of rows behind me so I got up and ran to sit on her knee from where I refused to be budged.

The time came for the infants' class to perform their dance. But would I leave my mother's knee? No. It took all of Miss McLeod's persuasive skills plus my mother's hefty shove on my bottom to persuade me to come out on to the dance floor and perform. I remember leading the others through the dance with a scowl on my face just to let everyone know I was doing it under duress.

I actually continued to attend the dance school for quite a few years, gaining my grade 3 ballet certificate and learning many Scottish country dances like the Eightsome Reel, the Highland Schottische and of course the Highland Fling. And I performed at all the annual balls with no trouble at all. Maybe I did learn quite a lot from that first traumatic public performance.

Milk Puddings and Me

I wanted apple dumpling,
but do you know what came?
Rice pudding.
Now isn't that a shame!
It isn't that I'm greedy
but oh it isn't nice
to hope for apple dumpling
and find it's only rice.

I learned this poem in primary school and it's stuck with me all these years because it reflects exactly how I feel. Substitute custard, sago, tapioca, semolina and any other milk pudding for rice and my sentiments remain the same. I hated them all. I would sit at the dinner table with a plate of the stuff in front of me, and sulk.

My mother was very keen to build me and my brother up. I suppose that after the war, when rationing was still in force, it must have been difficult for parents to ensure that their children received plenty of nourishing food. Yes, there was dried milk and dried egg that came in big tins (very useful for holding buttons, bits of jigsaws, kirby grips and other small items after they were empty) but they didn't do much to enhance the flavour of the meal.

To add to my mother's concerns I disliked milk intensely. I wouldn't drink it cold and certainly not hot when just the smell and the sight of the skin forming on top was enough to put me off. What I had been fed on as a baby I do not know, but I cannot remember a time when I did not detest milk.

But what are all these strange substances that are used to make milk puddings? Sago, tapioca and semolina are all forms of starch taken from plants; sago from the pith of tropical palms, tapioca from cassava roots and semolina is the coarse parts of various wheats and they are all cooked in similar ways. My *Glasgow Cookery Book* (1966 edition) has recipes for them all.

Semolina Pudding

1.5 ozs semolina

1 pint milk

1oz sugar

1egg

Heat the milk and sprinkle in the semolina. Bring to boiling point stirring all the time. (That was my job). Simmer for ten minutes. Add sugar.

This was as far as my mother's version went. She would then dish it up and dollop a spoonful of jam on top.

The recipe continues; beat egg and add carefully to pudding, stirring well. Pour into baking dish and bake till set. Personally, I don't think I would have liked it any better had she taken to time to complete the recipe as I didn't like eggs either.

The *Glasgow Cookery Book* has, as the recipe for sago pudding; *make as for semolina*. For tapioca pudding, *make as for sago pudding*. In other words they're all basically the same recipe. And all equally horrible.

Custard is different. It's made in two ways. My *Glasgow Cookery Book* gives a recipe for baked custard which requires two eggs, 1oz sugar, 1 pint milk and grated nutmeg. The eggs and sugar are beaten together, hot milk is stirred in and the whole lot poured into a dish with nutmeg sprinkled on top and baked for about 45 minutes till set.

And then there was my mother's version which was probably much more popular amongst busy housewives: put 2 tablespoons of custard powder and 1-2 tablespoons of sugar in a bowl.

Mix into a smooth paste with a little milk taken from 1 pint.

Heat the remaining milk to nearly boiling and pour onto the custard mix, stirring well. (My job again.)

Return to the saucepan and bring to the boil over a gentle heat, stirring continuously.

Alfred Bird invented egg-free custard powder in 1837 because his wife was allergic to eggs. He used cornflour instead of egg as the thickener and it was only when it was accidentally served to guests who enjoyed it, that he decided to produce it commercially. He followed it up with devising baking powder as his poor wife was also allergic to yeast and he could make a form of bread for her with it.

Lunchtime was when we had our main meal as everyone had lengthy breaks so they could get home for a meal. My father cycled home every lunch time for a main course followed by a dessert, more often than not a milk pudding. Sometimes there was a rice pudding which took forever in the oven. Rice, butter, sugar and milk were mixed together and baked for three hours till it was ready. Sometimes, cinnamon or nutmeg were sprinkled on top or my mother would add raisins to see if that would tempt me, but no, it didn't.

Funnily enough, I enjoyed all kinds of ice-cream, cones, sliders, 99s and bowls filled with the tally-man's own make. It's frozen milk basically, but I couldn't persuade my mother to accept that as a substitute milk pudding!

My younger brother adored milk puddings and tucked into all of them with gusto. His particular favourite was custard and as a special treat, he was usually allowed his favourite bit - the skin on the top. When he grew a bit older and was aware of my loathing for the stuff he would deliberately slurp up the skin just to annoy me, which it did.

Meanwhile I would sit there, stirring the spoonful of jam around and around in the pudding until the whole thing took on a pale pink shade if it was raspberry jam, or lilac if it was blackcurrant. Either way, it didn't taste any better. I remember the doctor calling in to see my brother and my mother reporting to him, as I sat on my own at the lunch table, everybody else having finished ages before, that I wouldn't eat up my milk pudding. Not even the doctor's remonstrations were sufficient to make me change my mind.

A milky drink at bedtime was another ruse my demented mother would try to get me to take the stuff. Ovaltine or drinking chocolate was served up in a cup at bedtime and carefully carried upstairs by me when we went to brush our teeth. By this time, the dreaded skin had formed on the top. Stirring it in just left bits of it floating around. As soon as my mother turned her back, the drink was tipped down the plughole followed by vigorous running of the cold tap to get rid of the evidence. Never was I so keen on brushing my teeth!

Family members, health visitors, friends all assured her that I would soon grow out of it. I have to report that no, I never did. I met a friend for coffee recently. She had arrived first and had a latte sitting ready for me. I somewhat vehemently informed her that I couldn't drink it as it was made with milk. I'm sure she thought I was a bit odd. I avoid all those fancy coffees you get nowadays, I don't eat trifle (it's got custard in it) and I never have a pudding if there's a chance they will pour custard over it. I prefer my apple dumpling without anything on it - except ice-cream of course!

Cards on the Table!

    Grandma Jane was a serious card player. Whist was her game and Whist Drives her passion. When it was her turn to host an afternoon one, it was all hands to the wheel. The house was scrubbed, the bathroom gleamed and the front room was rearranged to fit in as many of our folding card tables as possible. As she stayed with us, it meant my mother had to bake trays of scones to feed the large number of genteel ladies who turned up and kept their hats on throughout the proceedings.

Each card table had a pack of playing cards, a pencil and a pad for keeping scores. Chairs were commandeered from all over the house, including the stool from my mother's dressing table and the low nursing chair with several cushions on it to raise the occupant up.

Then the games began, games in the sense of Olympic when there is a great striving to win. So it was with those elderly ladies. We were kept well away from proceedings though we could hear the silences when play was ongoing, interspersed with the chat and occasional arguments when the rounds finished. After each one, players moved

Grannies and Grandpa with my mum and me.

round to the next table where new opponents were faced and the game began again. At the end, when the winner was declared, my role began. Carefully holding the sugar bowl, I made my way around the ladies to allow them to spoon it into their cups of tea. Tea and scones finished, they departed to catch their tram home, a tram stop being conveniently placed outside our house.

My mother and her four brothers all learned to play bridge at an early age and competition was fierce among them. Hands were replayed many times over in

23

discussion and arguments about failings in bidding common. When one of her younger brothers (aged 90) came over from South Africa to visit her many years later, the arguments began again and were just as vociferous.

When there was no-one to play with, Grandma Jane played various forms of Patience (or Solitaire as it's also known) She taught me to play them too but I never knew their names, though on the computer, where I still play them, they're known as Demon and Klondike and Canfield.

Ginny MacDonald was taught to play rummy by her Uncle Bob and Auntie Beattie. Bets were laid and the game began. To her surprise, at the end, she had won and had a healthy collection of pennies beside her. She assumed they would be returned to the kitty for the next time they played and was astonished when they insisted that she keep her winnings.

Liz McElhose also enjoyed 'betting', this time playing Newmarket. The kings were the 'horses' and 'bets', using matches, buttons or pennies, were placed on them. She also played a card game, a form of Old Maid, which her family called Scabby Annie, and which we called Rickety Annie or Crackit Aggie and which involved trying to pass on the Queen of Spades so that you weren't left with it when all the other cards were paired off.

My other grandmother, Grandma Kate, had a different approach to card and board games. Every Sunday afternoon, we all went to her house for high tea, a look at Grandpa George's beautiful garden and then an evening of games. The table was cleared, a large, thick baize cover was laid on it and the games began, games in the sense of laugh out loud, slapstick and hissy fits. One of our favourites was Stop the Bus, when you had to get as close to a score of 31 as possible. If you did score 31, you shouted Stop the Bus and the game finished immediately. The others had to give their scores and the lowest lost a 'life'. A match was removed from their tally of three and the first one to lose all three was kindly given 'charity' or another shot to try to stay in the game.

Pass the Penny was Grandpa George's speciality. Grandma Kate had a glass sugar bowl filled with old pennies just for games such as these, and pennies (one less than the number playing) were placed in a row in the centre of the table. Cards were removed from the pack so that there was a set of four for each player. On the command 'Cards on the table' you discarded a card you didn't want, and then on 'Pass!' you pushed it across to your neighbour on the left. You picked up the card passed to you, decided if you wanted to keep it and discarded another. If the commands came thick and fast, all your concentration was on checking your cards and we never noticed whenGrandpa George quietly put his four matching cards down and lifted one of the pennies. Then it was a battle to grab a penny before everyone else and the loser lost a life.

Grandma Kate didn't like serious games, especially if she was losing. Fortunately she had a large stack of packs of playing cards, as often, her losing hand was flung into

Grandma Kate and Grandpa George.

the coal fire and wasn't able to be retrieved before the flames destroyed them. She also enjoyed Johnnie's Lost His Coo, a riotous affair when the loser was subjected to whacks on the nose from the cards of the other players!

The board game we played most often was Ludo and if there were more than four players, we were split into teams. Then warfare began! Teams were allowed to form barriers when two or more of your counters landed on the same spot and doubled up to prevent other players passing while your colour scooted for the safety of home. Grandma Kate was inclined to lose her temper when caught behind a barrier for any length of time, and more than once, the board would be tossed in the air with the declaration that the game was a bogey!

Ken Stewart remembers playing Sorry! which he describes as a more vicious form of Ludo. Just as well Grandma Kate never played that! He also played Scoop! which involved competing journalists trying to fill their newspaper with stories.

Dominoes was a quieter activity if even more intense. We played with a set which had double nine as the biggest one, or 'Curny Wull' as he was known in our household, presumably derived from the number of spots looking like currants. Many people have claimed that a double six was the highest domino but Ken remembers his set having up to a double 12!

After the table was cleared, the games began.

If any of us couldn't play, then we 'chapped' or knocked, with a domino on the table. I used to like mixing up the dominoes in preparation for a new game when I would swirl them round on the polished table, the baize cover having been removed for that particular game.

Every Sunday, Ginny and her brother were taken to visit their great-aunt Nellie. It was not a cheery occasion as Aunt Nellie was a member of a religious group which banned the playing of games on the Sabbath. So they had to sit with a set of Chinese Chequers and a tea towel which was used to cover the game any time they suspected that Aunt Nellie was on the prowl.

Nowadays, games are on laptops and phones and are just not the same as face to face fun!

Our Christmas in the 1950's

Christmas was coming. As the great day neared, my brother and I asked for some paper and pencils and penned our annual letters to Santa. Great thought went into their composition. After enquiring after his health, there followed the most important part - what we would like as a present. One item and one item only was the rule though we always added 'and a surprise' just in case he was feeling generous.

The letter signed and sealed, the next part was to send it to Santa. This was a serious business. Not for us the posting it in a letterbox addressed to Lapland or the North Pole, we had a direct and somewhat magical connection to him. The fire would be blazing brightly in the living room, the brass fire irons hanging from their stand in the hearth. My father would take up the poker and, knocking it firmly against the chimney breast, he would shout up 'Are you there Santa?' Perhaps the first time Santa wasn't, or didn't hear or was too busy with other boys and girls all sending him their messages, so Dad would knock again.

Eventually Dad would give us a nod to let us know Santa was listening, and carefully, oh so carefully, we would toss our letters into the fire. It was always an exciting moment watching the paper blacken and curl and then burst into flames. We were satisfied. The letters were on their way to Santa.

Then, as Christmas crept oh, so slowly nearer, we had to make sure that Santa remembered what we'd asked for, so Dad would take us in the tram to the centre of Glasgow to one of the big department stores, Copland and Lye, Pettigrew and Stephens or Lewis's and visit Santa there.

There was always a long queue on the Saturday before Christmas but we waited patiently until at last, it was our turn to sit on his knee and whisper into his ear. A nod of his head, a wee parcel from his elf beside him and it was all over. Now all we had to do was to wait till Christmas came.

On Christmas Eve, we hung up our stockings on a string along the mantelpiece. Dad's long, thick hand-knitted (by Grandma Jane) stockings which he used for cycling were ideal; they were very large and they stretched! Plenty of room for presents in them. Just so Santa would know which was which, a photo of each of us was pinned to the top.

Then there was the wee glass of sherry and a plate with a few iced diamond biscuits to sustain him on his busy night's work. They were set carefully on the hearth for him to see when he came down the chimney.

Of course, we couldn't get to sleep, it was all too exciting. On more than one occasion, my mother had to shoo us back up the stairs to bed as they, unknown to us, were in the process of filling the stockings and had not yet gone to bed.

But eventually, it was Christmas Day and, wrapped up in our dressing gowns and warm slippers against the cold of an unheated house, we dashed down the stairs and into the living room. A wondrous sight greeted us. Santa had been! Ripping off paper, we exclaimed over our gifts. Some were the same every year; a new pair of slippers for our growing feet, a ten shilling note in an envelope for our savings, a novelty bar of soap and, right at the foot of the stocking, a tangerine. We spent Christmas morning happily playing with our new toys and wearing our new slippers.

In the afternoon, we dressed in our party clothes and headed for our other grandparents in Drumoyne. We took the number 23 bus and walked round the corner to their house in Carleith Quadrant. We had a high tea there and one

picture shows us tucking into what looks suspiciously like tinned spaghetti. But that would have been a treat for us and one we thoroughly enjoyed. Grandma Kate always made sure there was plenty of cake and sweets and we would return home tired and feeling just a bit sick.

The next day, Boxing Day, the fun continued. Dad would take us to the Kelvin Hall Circus and Carnival. After marvelling at clowns, elephants, acrobats and the lion tamer, it would be time for a shot on the Helter-Skelter and the Dodgems and, my scary favourite, the Ghost Train. We ate lurid pink candy floss and drank fizzy pop. For the second day running, we returned home, tired and feeling just a bit sick, and perhaps secretly glad that the celebrations were over for another year.

Brrr! Winter's Here Again!

We must have been far hardier in our youth as regards the cold. After all, we just had to put up with it.

I remember those beautiful frost pictures on the windows which we used to waken

My first taste of snow.

up to on many a winter's morning. And the milk on the doorstep often had a frozen top of cream pushing up the cap.

Shirts and underwear came in from the washing line rigid with ice to drip forlornly on the pulley. We'd walk all the way to school, arriving with bare, red knees and feeling the agony of warmth returning to frozen toes in wellingtons.

I always envied people who lived in single ends, those one-room homes which now would be called studio flats. At least they were warm with the big black range on the go most of the time to heat water, cook meals, help dry the washing hanging from the pulley and provide a level of warmth not found in other, larger houses.

Once a week the coal man would march up the close stairs carrying a hundredweight of coal on his back and empty his sack in the bunker conveniently sited beside the table where you ate or the sideboard where the dishes were stored. The dust went everywhere despite the covering of newspapers spread over surfaces and woe betide any housewife who still had washing drying when he arrived. Nothing for it but down to the wash-house again with the now sooty underwear.

Bigger houses usually had coal fires in the main rooms but generally only one was lit. Every morning the ashes from the previous day had to be scraped out, saving the larger cinder lumps to help light the fire. Then yesterday's newspaper was separated out into sheets which were rolled up into tubes and twisted into pretzel shapes. Other people merely scrunched the paper up but my granny was convinced that our special rolled paper helped get the fire going well. On top of the paper were laid kindling

sticks, bought in bundles from the hardware store, and then the cinders followed by a lump or two of the precious coal. A match was lit, and you waited with baited breath to see if the fire would catch. If it didn't, and simply sputtered out, then it was a case of starting all over again, refining the placement of the various components so that with a bit of luck, it took.

That was generally the only heating in the house so most activities took place there, especially in the evenings when the cold seeped in through the many cracks and crevices and ill-fitting windows. We would sit as close to the fire as possible while our backs were still frozen and our bare legs were scorched. 'Corned beef' legs, as the red blotchy marks were called, were common then.

In one old house we lived in, the kitchen and scullery were far from the front of the house, so in order to prevent my mother developing hypothermia while she was cooking, my father bought a paraffin heater. This sat in the middle of the kitchen and provided a small circle of warmth. Unfortunately, one day my mother, carrying a huge basket of washing in from the line, kicked it over and started a somewhat scary fire which my father had to rush through to put out.

Even after I was married and had a brand new flat in a new town in the 1960's, the only heating supplied was an ugly big storage heater in the main room which randomly gave out heat when you least needed it; the rest of the flat was just as cold as before. We certainly didn't need a fridge in the kitchen to keep food cool as the cupboard with the vent to the outside did the job excellently.

Toilets and bathrooms were so cold that baths were infrequent and constipation common. Those with toilets on the 'stair heid' usually kept a chanty or potty under the bed to save nocturnal visits out to the toilet in your bare feet. The toilet blocks in school were frequently outside so that every time there was a cold spell and the water in them froze, we had to be sent home. Most children looked forward to that aspect of the winter.

Having a bath was a massive operation. Firstly, there was the problem of making sure there was enough hot water. Some lucky folk had a boiler behind the coal fire which heated water, others had an immerser which was only switched on for that purpose, it being too expensive otherwise. Most times, the available hot water filled only a quarter of the bath and usually was shared with the other children in the family and after, by parents if it wasn't too cold by then. Those without baths could visit the local steamie and wallow in plentiful hot water in the hot baths provided there.

Otherwise it was just a quick 'dicht' with a cloth over your hands and face, an

equally quick scrub of your teeth and a dash into the freezing bedroom and into your pyjamas and the bliss of discovering a hot water bottle in your bed!

Again, I envied those in single ends and room-and-kitchens with the box bed in the kitchen. Not only was it warmer there but you could listen into the adults' conversation while pretending to be asleep.

There were no such things as duvets then; instead there were many layers of blankets topped by a quilt if you were lucky, the whole lot weighing you down and trapping you in your bed. Granny patiently sewed the scraps from her dressmaking into large patchwork squares which she folded in half around an old thin blanket long past its best, to make a bed cover. They were made to last and I still have one she made over 60 years ago.

We dressed for the cold in layers of clothing; first a cotton vest followed by a liberty bodice, a fleecy garment with fastenings on the front. Then a blouse or shirt with a hand-knitted woolly jumper on top. Boys wore short trousers all year round while we

Dressed for the cold.

had thick tweed skirts. Hand-knitted long socks up to our knees were held in place by garters, usually a piece of broad elastic sewn just that bit too tight so that you had red welts around your legs when you took them off.

Coats were heavy and made for your growth and always with your mittens on a long string running up the sleeve, across the shoulders and down the other side. Boys wore caps and girls pixie hats, again hand-knitted. It wasn't exactly lightweight clothing nor was it waterproof.

As a teenager, I perfected the art of dressing under the bedclothes on winter mornings so that I would throw back the bedclothes and emerge ready for the day, fully dressed in my school uniform though it was a bit crushed.

Would I go back to those cold days? No, definitely not. With a climate like ours we need all the creature comforts going!

Toys Built to Last

Toys were precious. There weren't so many as nowadays, but they were made to last. In our house, toys were demarcated along gender lines; I played with dolls, my brother with cars. I wasn't interested in his cars and he certainly wasn't interested in

My favourite doll, Mary, all the way from South Africa.

my dolls.

I had several dolls; Rosemary and Margaret were made of a hard, moulded material but had moving arms and legs and their eyes could open and shut when you tipped them backwards and forwards. My grandmother knitted beautiful little outfits for them. I remember a particularly pretty one of a coat, leggings and a beret in a soft rose wool. Then there was Wendy who had hair, real long blonde hair!

But my favourite was Mary, a black felt doll that my gallivanting granny had brought back from one of her trips to South Africa where one of her sons and his family lived. Mary was different and soft and hence much more comfortable in bed. She didn't stick into you when you turned over.

My brother loved his Meccano set, thin metal bars of varying lengths with holes in them into which you screwed tiny nuts and bolts to join them together. Very fiddly but satisfying when you finally managed it. He added to his set over the years,

building all sorts of strange vehicles and structures. I remember a crane which had a working pulley on it. He subscribed to Meccano Magazine for many years and collected a huge pile of copies which he still has. No doubt they're worth something now.

I loved playing with my post office set which included miniature envelopes and writing paper, toy stamps and even a rubber stamp and ink pad to frank the envelopes. And my baking set had a mini size rolling pin which my mother commandeered as it was just the right size to roll out her scone mix.

A play shop had a cash register with coins, scales for weighing dry goods (beans and raisins supplied by mum) and small brown paper bags to put them in. There were also tiny cardboard packets purporting to contain gravy mix, sugar and salt. We

played for hours with it.

A train set was something I didn't get much chance to operate as my brother prized it greatly. He would spend hours on the carpet setting up his trains and the rails. They were metal and slotted into each other and could make a circle or lead off into a siding. More time was spent putting it all together than in actually operating it.

There was a radiogram on which we used to listen to the children's programmes. When we were small, every day at a quarter to two, *Listen with Mother* would have us squashing into an armchair either side of my mother to listen. The presenter would say 'Are you sitting comfortably? Then I'll begin.' We had fifteen minutes of such stirring songs as *Hob Shoe Hob* and *Here We Go Round the Mulberry Bush*. After the story came the sleepy music (the *Berceuse* from Fauré's Dolly Suite) which was supposed to accompany us to our afternoon nap but the only person who fell asleep was my mother. Later, we became devotees of *Children's Hour*.

We were left to make our own entertainment most of the time. We dressed up like all children in whatever we could find and played games in the garden. An old cold frame became a boat in which we sailed all over the world and about which we wrote a lengthy poem to rival the Odyssey.

We also wrote our own musical plays and performed them in a miniature theatre made out of a shoe box. We painted the backdrops, made curtains and costumes out of crepe paper and used my little ballet figurines as actors. The plays were mainly our retelling of fairy stories such as Cinderella and Red Riding Hood, but they provided us with hours of fun and the adults with much mirth when we performed

them. They weren't supposed to be comedies and we couldn't understand why they laughed so much but, as we were usually rewarded with sixpence or a shilling, we didn't mind.

My brother's most favourite toy of all was his pedal car in the style of an American army jeep. The pace of our Sunday afternoon walks was set by his pedalling as fast as he could and being pushed up hills on it. I had a red trike which could go much faster than him except downhill when I would apply the brakes and, as he had none, he would shoot past me, hoping that there wasn't a bend or a pothole to upend him.

But best of all were my books. We had all the Noddy books, brightly coloured and such a change from *My First Enid Blyton Book*, which was indeed my first one and very wordy it was too. No five year old would thank you for it nowadays but there were not many children's books available then. 'A Day in Fairyland' was another favourite. A Christmas present, it was twice as large as any other book and filled with

pretty illustrations of fairies going about their daily lives.

We kept our books in an old orange box covered with some of the leftover wallpaper from our bedroom - little pink and blue flowers, my choice obviously. The rest of our toys were stored on two shelves in the living room press (cupboard) and the tricycle and jeep in the garden hut. But wherever they were kept, they were precious to us and we had such good fun with them all.

A go at the train set

Dressing up.

My trike and my brother's jeep.

Awa' Tae Bide Awa'

Scarcely a family in Scotland does not have relatives who have made the move overseas. From the times of the Highland Clearances in the eighteenth and nineteenth centuries onwards, the Scots have moved abroad, either forcibly at the hands of landowners or voluntarily in the search for a better life. Apparently there are now more Scots or descendants of Scots living in the traditional diaspora destinations of North America and Australasia than in Scotland itself.

My family are typical of many others. In the nineteenth century, they moved south from Tain to Glasgow to seek work in the industrial areas there, the shipyards and the steel works. Others came across from the Isle of Arran where Robin McKelvie had been a captain of a puffer, again to seek work in Glasgow. But in the 1920's and 30's in the days after the First World War and the Depression, they spread their wings and headed across the Atlantic to North America.

Great-aunt Polly and family with the winter log pile,
Saskatchewan, Canada 1930s.

Great-aunt Polly sailed for Canada and the prairies of Saskatchewan. I can only imagine the shock she must have experienced at the sight of the flat lands stretching for miles in every direction and the long, bitterly cold winters. Great-aunt Jessie lived in New Jersey while Great-aunt Robina ended up as a nanny in Connecticut after her husband was killed in the First World War.

During the Second World War, one of my uncles who was in the Royal Navy, called in at Cape Town and was entranced by what he saw there. As soon as he was discharged after the war, he took his family off to South Africa, except it wasn't the balmy shores of the Cape they went to but a dry, dusty mining town many hundreds of miles inland.

Great-aunt Jessie and family, South Carolina 1953.

So during my childhood there was a constant stream of airmail letters flying backwards and forwards every week. My mother had to roll up the 'Sunday Post' in the special brown wrapping for posting newspapers so that those overseas would get their weekly dose of the Broons and Oor Wullie, Francis Gay and the Hon Man.

What I really enjoyed was the food parcels which would arrive from our American relations after the war when rationing was even tighter than before. Tins of ham and fruit cocktail and best of all, packets of dried chicken noodle soup, a wonderful invention! Just add hot water and hey presto chicken noodle soup! And what a soup! So different from the homemade variety, thick with lentils and dried peas and barley and a piece of hough. I can still taste that American soup, slightly salty with a flavour new to my palate, fresh and savoury and absolutely delicious. No present day chicken noodle soup quite matches it.

They also sent clothes as they were still rationed too. I remember in particular a fetching outfit in navy blue trimmed with red; it had a dress with a straight skirt, cap sleeves and a matching mini cape which tied round the shoulders. Very elegant and so American! Fortunately it was too big for me as it wouldn't have gone down so well in the streets of Glasgow but it was great fun using it for dressing up in.

In the 1950's the relatives made visits home. They were an exotic breed with their strange accents, neither broad American as in the movies but not Scots either. I remember Aunt Polly's favourite exclamation 'Good night' as in 'Good night, I can't find my gloves!'

They spoke of wonders like huge refrigerators and massive automatic cars, central heating and hot showers. In America, they ate things like corn on the cob and grits and hamburgers and while here, spooned home-made strawberry jam on to their plate of bacon and eggs that my mother cooked for them. I don't know how they felt being back in the old country, but they never visited home again.

In the 50s and 60s Australia became popular with the introduction of the £10 fare. For that sum per adult, a family could enjoy a six week trip out to Australia and get help to settle when they got there. Except like everything in life, it wasn't all it was cracked up to be. The earliest immigrants complained the the ship's food was too rich after the severe rationing of the war years and beyond, many were seasick and there wasn't much on board for families with young children to do to keep them entertained. And of course there was always the danger of them falling overboard.

Pauline remembers the headlines in the local paper of her small town when they were one of five families from the area to emigrate; Mass Exodus to Australia! it read. They sailed through the Suez canal at the time of the Suez crisis and there were British soldiers standing on shore to ensure safe passage of the ship, the SS Himalaya. When they reached Melbourne, both she and her parents were overtaken by fear at the enormity of what they had done in coming to this strange land.

My own exodus came in 1969 when my husband and I left to sail to Canada. The train to the Liverpool docks where the SS Empress of England was waiting, left from Glasgow's Central Station. The family were gathered on the platform to wave us off, stiff upper lips to the fore as we were not a family given to displays of emotion. We stood at the window as the train pulled, oh so slowly, away from the platform, our hearts bursting, the tears threatening to spill over in floods. And that was knowing that we would see them all again within a year when plans were afoot for them to join a

My first taste of skiing, Quebec, Canada 1970

'travel club', charter a plane and fly over to see us. I can only imagine the distress many of the earlier emigrants must have felt, when the prospects of seeing their families again were negligible.

And like many emigrants before, the experience of sailing across the Atlantic was not all fun and games. Seasickness prevailed, despite reassurances from the crew that it wasn't rough enough to switch on the stabilisers. However, we did meet up with several other young couples off to seek jobs and adventure in the new world. We stayed in the home of my husband's head teacher for a few days and it was then I came across my first cantaloupe. I had no idea what it was, fruit or vegetable, nor what to do with it. The apples and tomatoes were another source of amazement, being very large and very juicy. In fact, a trip to the local supermarket was like entering Aladdin's cave, stuffed full of all sorts of wonderful foods.

It's only since the Second World War that emigrants have had the option of returning home if they could afford it. After two years in Australia, families could return to the UK without having to repay the full cost of their trip out. And almost a quarter of them did for a variety of reasons, lack of jobs, family not settling, homesickness. Still, that's a lot of families who remained to make a new home away from Scotland.

Over the Sea

Every year when we were small, my mother would either rent a tenement flat in Millport or a house on the Isle of Arran and we'd decamp there for a month. The holiday would start with the train journey from Glasgow to the coast, usually Fairlie or Largs, where we would wait for the boat across to the Isle of Cumbrae and the wee town of Millport, or a bigger boat for the sail to Arran.

We knew the names of all the boats which would call in at the pier where we waited and would try to guess which one would be ours. There was the Wee Cumbrae and the

Maids, (two wee ships called Ashton and Leven), all heading for Millport and larger vessels like the Talisman and the Marchionesses of Graham and Lorne for longer trips across the Firth of Clyde.

While waiting we would play on the gangplanks which we called 'gangwangs', walking across them till they tilted, and then back to tilt them the other way. The pier workers were very patient with us, only yelling at us to get off them when the constant bang! bang! annoyed them or when the boat was coming.

We weren't good travellers, my brother being seasick before the boat had even left the pier on one memorable occasion, so my mother usually tried to pick the shortest crossing rather than sailing all the way 'doon the watter' from Glasgow.

But I loved the sail, whether to Millport or Brodick on Arran. The first thing on boarding was to get a good seat, out of the wind and the smoke and if possible, in the sunshine. (I don't remember any wet trips!) Then out came the sandwiches the minute the boat left the pier and the seagulls gathered at the stern. Crusts were saved for them and they would swoop perilously close to us and snatch them from our fingers. Sometimes a finger felt the snap of their beaks on them!

While we ate, an accordion band played Scottish dance tunes and songs, and we sometimes joined in the choruses. Then the band would move off to another part of the ship, playing all the way. Watching the white foam of the ship's wake from the stern of the ship was another pastime and being held up on the rails gave us a thrill as well as a good vantage point.

Another tradition was the trip down to the engine room to see the engines. Massive cranks and pistons roared up and down propelling the boat on its journey. It was

48

mesmerising to watch but the noise was deafening and the fumes strong, so it was back up on deck again to breathe the fresh salt air and watch as we neared our destination. Carefully, the boat would manoeuvre itself till it was side on to the pier, and the sailors at the bow and stern would fling the ropes, always accurately, to the men there. They heaved the heavy loops of rope over the bollards and gradually the ship would come to a stop right at the edge, close enough for the gangplanks to reach.

We all trooped off, breathed in the holiday air, and set off to our temporary home. We had arrived.

The Govan Fair

The excitement was mounting. Folk craned their heads down the road watching for the first signs. I clutched the faded red plush cushion as I leaned out the window, waiting, waiting. At last, a ripple moved through the crowd.

'It's coming, it's coming.' In the distance we could hear the band and then through the crowds packed on either side of the street, came the Ram's Head. The Govan Fair had started.

When I was wee, it was almost a tradition that Grandma Jane took my younger brother and I on the 23 bus to Govan the first Friday evening in June. We were going to visit Grandma Jane's friends, Bella and Mima Smith who lived up a close on Langlands Road. They had a room and kitchen one stair up above Hailstones' fish shop where Bella had worked until she sliced her finger filleting a haddie. It was a perfect site to view the Govan Fair pass by.

There was always the same strange smell peculiar to their home, a mixture of close living, gas lighting and cheap perfume. (Mima's – she was a business lady and went out to work in an office up the town and had had the same boyfriend for over twenty years). I always associate that heavy odour with the Fair. It added to my rising excitement to smell it as we stepped into their lobby.

But first there were pleasantries to get through, the enquiries after mutual acquaintances and family. The voices would drop at any news of a gynaecological nature – although I was too young to understand the nods and meeting of eyes I was keen to know what they were discussing and listened intently while pretending to be doing anything but. All the time, the waiting, the waiting.

Eventually the three women agreed that the time was right for the opening of the two front windows. Kitty the cat was removed from her usual perch on the ledge and the sashes were thrown up as high as they could go. The faded red plush cushions were lifted from the old settee and chairs from ben the room brought in. Being wee, we were given the cushions to hing out on, above the milling crowds who had nothing like as good a view as we did. I was always scared my cushion would plummet out into the street and I hung on to it like a life belt.

Mima always gave us a pile of pennies and ha'pennies to fling out to the floats and this, balanced precariously on the window ledge beside my cushion, ensured my virtual immobility.

I remember it as being warm and dry though that couldn't always have been the case. Perhaps the rosy childhood memories have edited out any dreich, damp evenings.

At last, at long, endless last, the Ram's Head appeared into view carried on high by the man leading the procession. Behind him was a band, one of many, all competing to drown out the rest. Then the Govan Queen's car slowly moved forward. There she sat,

All dressed up for the Govan Fair.

wearing a long white dress with a cloak draped in ermine and so brightly red it dazzled me. Her head held high, she balanced the crown just recently placed there in the ceremony in the Elderpark.

That was my ambition. To be the Queen of Govan Fair. To be crowned on a throne in Elderpark by a local worthy's wife and then to ride in that car with my ermine cloak spread out behind me. To wave my acknowledgement to the crowds. To smile and have my picture in the Govan Press.

Everything else that passed after the Queen did not hold my attention as much. I threw my pennies as best I could. I remember my embarrassment when one of my pennies missed its target and hit a man standing underneath me right on his head. He rubbed the spot and turned to look up to where it had come from. I slunk in from the window afraid he might realise I was the culprit and run up the close to chastise me.

Floats from all the works in the area drove slowly past, sometimes stopping as the crowds pushed forward. I once saw my big cousin sitting on a float from the Govan High School choir. She stuck out because while all the other girls were standing waving and shouting at the crowds, she alone sat huddled in a corner looking miserable and discomfited.

The last float passed by and the crowds pushed on to the road and began making their way home. Bella went ben the hoose and put the kettle on. We always had a cup of tea while the crowds dispersed. Then Grandma Jane gathered us together and we made our way along Langlands Road to Govan Cross and stood waiting for the number 23 bus home.

Sadly, I was never the Queen of Govan Fair.

Holidays in Millport

Most summers my mother would rent a room and kitchen in Barend Street, Millport, on the Isle of Cumbrae, for the month of July. My mother, brother and I plus one of my grannies would squeeze ourselves into this tiny flat. It was pretty basic with a box bed in the kitchen recess, a black-leaded range to cook on and gas lighting. Fortunately, in the long summer evenings, we didn't need to light the lamps too often. I can still remember the pop-popping sound as they were lit and how careful my mother had to be when handling the delicate gas mantles.

There was no bathroom, only a shared toilet out on the stair landing. Our toilet paper, Izal Germicide of course, had a loop of string through the roll and this was hung on the handle of the kitchen door. When paying a visit to the toilet, you first tore off a couple of slices of it to take with you.

However such inconveniences didn't bother us; after all we were on holiday! The first necessity was to buy a new tin pail and spade for making sand-pies with. This was a serious business as each year we were promoted to a larger size of decorated pail and a longer wooden spade. Then down to the sands of Kames Bay to build castles and pies to our hearts' content while the grown-ups sheltered out of the wind.

Every morning my brother and I were sent to the local bakery for fresh morning rolls. Clutching the bag of still warm rolls, we would hurry back to have them for our breakfast. It was also our job to collect the milk from the dairy. Carrying the milk can, we would make the short walk round to the farm where the dairy was situated. There, the lady poured the fresh milk from her big can into our little one, pop the lid on top and then we would set off back home with it, making sure we didn't spill a drop.

Another important part of the holiday was renting push bikes and tricycles to pedal about the roads, sometimes even all round the the island, a distance of just over ten miles. The almost traffic free main road was perfect for youngsters and the not so young to cycle around, mainly anti-clockwise in our case. There was much to see on our journey; first the crocodile rock on the foreshore which the council kept painted with a red mouth, white teeth and a big red and white eye to make it even more life-like. Then further along Kames Bay, there was the lion rock where I must confess, I never really was able to make out the lion. Turning into the wind along the east facing side of the island we eventually came to the marine station near Keppel pier where scientists researched the sea life around the coast.

One of my most favourite places to visit was the Garrison. The Garrison House was originally built to house soldiers engaged on Customs and Excise duties, i.e. keeping an eye out for smugglers who were very common along Cumbrae's coastline! The extensive grounds were now open to the public to wander round the parkland and enjoy the amenities. There was a flat concreted area where little tin horses were for hire and I loved going up and down on one of them. You pushed down on both pedals at the same time and this moved the horse forwards and up and down just like I imagined a real horse would do.

The swings, roundabout and seesaw in the children's play-park at the other end of the town was another place we frequented and much fun we had there. We made many new friends among the children of the regular holiday-makers from the West of Scotland who returned year after year to the island.

Everybody came to Millport or so it seemed as friends and relatives joined us from Glasgow especially during the Glasgow Fair Fortnight at the end of July. Then, many factories and businesses closed for two whole weeks and everyone had a holiday. My father joined us then so the flat was extremely full.

We liked going down to the pier to watch the paddle steamers arrive with another load of holiday-makers and day-trippers. It was a complicated job to get the ship to dock just at the right place so that the seamen could fling the ropes across to the men on the pier. They would catch the thinner length of rope and then begin the task of hauling the heavier ropes with the noose on the end till they were able to loop them over the bollards on the pier, one at the bow of the ship and one at the stern. The crew on the ship would wind in any slack in the ropes and then the gangways were pushed into position, fastened securely, and the passengers could disembark. I always had mixed feelings meeting the boats as I was always on the look-out for friends arriving but at the same time, I had to say goodbye to others.

On a quiet day, when we were older, we would fish off the end of the pier, hanging over the edge in anticipation of a catch, dangling our hooks baited with the contents of periwinkle shells and spending many happy hours trying to hook a tiddler. The seagulls

Everyone went to Millport.

watched us carefully in the hope that we would, as they would swoop down and attempt to steal our catch from us.

I don't remember the weather ever spoiling our enjoyment. When it was fine and there was a wee blink of sun, it was down to the beach to play on the sands building sandcastles surrounded by moats and topped with sand-pies, and even to venture into the chilly waters of the Firth of Clyde. I actually learned to swim there, a spluttering, splashy breast-stroke cum doggy paddle.

Colder, wetter weather saw us hiring bikes and pedalling as fast as we could around the town and further afield. That way we could keep warm as well. We met up with family and friends for picnics on grassy slopes with views across to the mainland, where we all shared the sandwiches and buns our mothers had brought.

I was always sad when it became time to pack up the hamper with our dirty clothes and all the sheets and towels we'd brought and send it back home, where it arrived several days after us. Returning home meant that the school holidays were almost over and back to school I would have to go - until the next year when we would once again sail back to Millport.

Family Biking

My parents were both keen cyclists in the 1930s, touring the country from Cape Wrath to Devon on their bikes. They eventually progressed to a tandem, one of the best, an FH Grubb Pullman. In 1937 my father was full of praise for this machine, writing in his journal of trips made that year:

'I pay tribute to FH Grubb, the brain behind the making of my tandem. Now well into its third year, it has carried me over 12,000 miles, as far north as Fort William, south to Cornwall....through fair weather and foul.'

Not only did World War Two put a dampener on their travels, so did the arrival of myself and my younger brother. Taking young children on a bike wasn't as easy as it is nowadays. There were only a few seats made to attach to cycles back then and they were expensive, so nothing daunted, my father decided to make his own.

My brother's seat on the tandem.

There were several attempts. Out in his workshop he hammered and welded, helped along by some of his more skilful cronies. He was an industrial chemist and a keen amateur photographer and his workshop doubled as a dark room for developing and enlarging his photographs. There were rows of shelves filled with large bottles of chemicals, trays of developing fluid and water, and little room to move, but this was where he endeavoured to create a child seat for a tandem.

The photo shows one of the later models and it looks as if has been made of something akin to Meccano. There are no straps holding my brother in and no sides to the seat, which is why he looks as if he's sitting in mid-air, with not much room for my mother. How she managed to cycle with a large child in front of her, I don't know. Perhaps this was just for my brother to accompany Dad on a boy's day out.

One of the very fancy seat models he made had a set of pedals attached so that my brother could imagine that he was contributing to the effort needed to get up hills. Was there a seat for me strapped on the back where the saddle bags went? I honestly can't remember.

What I do remember only too clearly was Dad's piece de resistance - he acquired an old sidecar from a motorbike and set to work on it. Somehow he attached it to the frame of the tandem with just enough space to allow my parents to pedal. We were plonked

Me in the sidecar.

into it and away we all went. There we were, sitting six inches above the ground, with no straps holding us in, no safety helmets, Dad's dodgy welding and a tendency not to want to turn corners. Health and Safety didn't enter into it. Fortunately we never did a Wallace and Gromit and separate mid-journey.

I remember a photo of my mother and me outside Inverbeg Youth Hostel on Loch Lomond. My mother is wearing her thick brown corduroy cycling shorts so we must have come by bike. Again I can't remember, so I suspect I kept my eyes shut throughout

Inverbeg Hostel.

the journey or was mesmerised by the sight of my father's muscly legs encased in beige, hand-knitted, ribbed long socks.

Travelling in the sidecar didn't last for long. We grew too big and at one point, refused to go anywhere near it. Perhaps we were more conscious of our safety than Dad was.

Nowadays a contraption like this would be banned. Such behaviour on the part of Mum and Dad would have the social work department rushing to rescue us from such reckless parenting. But we survived to tell the tale!

At the Sign of the Wee Red Triangle

I always enjoyed geography at school especially when we were given maps and asked to identify the symbols used. I was always able to pick out the wee red triangle as the site of a youth hostel. I was very familiar with the symbol as in our house, we all had membership cards for the Scottish Youth Hostelling Association and their logo of a red triangle with the letters SYHA inscribed in it.

The first Scottish youth hostel was opened in 1931 at Broadmeadows near Selkirk. It cost 1/- (5p) a night to stay in a dormitory with bunk beds, and cooking and washing facilities. The hostels were for hikers and cyclists only and those touring using a motor-car were not admitted. The number of hostels expanded until 1939 when war intervened and many hostellers were otherwise engaged in the war effort and holidaying was discouraged.

I have my mother's membership card from when she first joined in March 1938. It is in her maiden name and gives her address in Govan. Each year on payment of the membership fee (2/6d or 12.5p) a sticker was added to the front. Every time the card ran out of space for the hostel stamp showing they had spent a night there, another sheet was added. It became a matter of pride among hostellers to possess a battered old card, with a thick layer of membership stickers on the front and pages of hostel stamps inside! My mother's went through several incarnations including changing her name to

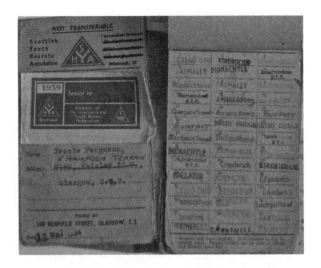 

her married one and various changes of address. Eventually the card became so battered and thick with additions that a new one was issued in 1956. Her last one, issued in 1963, still has her original photo from 1938, carefully removed from her original card and transferred to the new. And why not!

I became a member as soon as I was allowed to at the age of 5. We didn't go on long trips but visited Inverbeg on Loch Lomond and Killin, Garth and Strathtummel in the Trossachs. As far as I was concerned, the best part was getting to sleep on the top bunk. As soon as we arrived (always after 4pm when the hostel re-opened) and had handed our cards to the warden with our fee, it was into the women's dormitory and the job of bed-making began. Easy enough as it consisted of spreading out the cotton sleeping bag on the thin striped mattress and covering it with a couple of iron-grey rough blankets, making sure they were well tucked in in case I turned over and fell out.

Then to the kitchen where our metal cups, plates and cutlery were safely stowed in a wooden pigeon-hole specially for the purpose. Some hostel kitchens had long gas stoves but others had ranges with wood burning stoves providing the heat to cook on. Wanlockhead hostel was popular because it had a magnificent Aga which not only provided cooking space but heated the hostel as well.

As the number of hostellers arriving increased as the day waned, so did the demand for cooking space. After a day's cycling or hiking, the first thing everyone wanted was a good hot meal and plenty of it. Pots and pans were supplied and the frying pans always disappeared first as bacon, sausages, eggs (bought from the warden) and tattie scones were fried up for a quick and satisfying meal. Stories of how many miles hiked or cycled were exchanged over the communal tables as they tucked in. Then the queue to wash the dishes began. Not that there were many; the hostel's frying pan, one plate, tin mug, and knife and fork which went back in your pigeonhole ready for breakfast the next day.

After the meal, the hostellers congregated around the open fire in the common room to chat and exchange tales of journeys made and mountains climbed. As there was no TV or radio, entertainment was home-made and sing-songs were popular. Sometimes there was an old battered piano in the corner and anyone who could bash out a few tunes was encouraged to do so.

After 10pm the move to the dormitories began. Lights out was at 11pm and no warden would tolerate any noise after this time. If anyone had gone to the local pub (alcohol was not permitted in the hostels) which was sometimes a considerable distance away, and underestimated the time taken to get back to the hostel, then the wrath of the warden descended upon them and they were reported to the Behaviour Committee. My father, Bill Ferguson, was chair of this committee for many years and had to deal with such miscreants, the ultimate punishment being the removal of their hostelling membership.

The rules were printed on the back of everybody's membership card so there was no excuse for not knowing them.

Smoking in dormitories is prohibited; Gambling and the consumption of alcohol in Hostels is forbidden; Dogs are not admitted.

Beds must be prepared by 10pm; No cooking is allowed after 10.30pm; Lights must be out by 11pm.

(the warden usually had a master switch which enforced this!)

Silence must be observed from 11pm to 7am; hostellers must be out of bed by 9am.

(no long lies allowed!)

In the morning, after squeezing in to the basins to have a cursory wash in the usually cold water, breakfast was often again another fry up to keep energy levels high for the day ahead. The beds were stripped and blankets folded ready for the next occupant and you reported to the warden for your duty. Hostellers were expected to keep the hostels clean themselves and the warden would dole out tasks as he (or she) saw fit. I always seemed to get the job of sweeping a floor or two with a brush that was twice my size. Other tasks were chopping wood for the fires, cleaning the wash-basins or tidying the

A drum-up on the way....

kitchen. However if the warden didn't like you or you had broken one of the rules, then the task of cleaning the toilets was handed to you for your sins.

Everyone had left by 11am when the hostel closed till 4pm regardless of the weather. The warden had a few hours to himself till the next lot of hostellers turned up. Staying for more than two nights in the one hostel was frowned upon and you were expected to

...and the washing-up after.

head off either home at the end of the weekend, or further on to another hostel on your itinerary.

The SYHA was set up to encourage young people from the smoky, dirty cities to get out into the fresh air of the countryside and this they did in droves until the advent of the package holiday in the 60s. But the hostelling movement has kept up with people's higher expectations nowadays, providing family rooms and ensuite facilities and still the youngsters (and the not so young) come to stay at the sign of the wee red triangle. And yes, they even accept cars now!

Shopping Bags Rule Again!

It's funny how things come full circle. We're again learning the art of taking a shopping bag or bags with us when we go to the supermarket or clothes store. Here in Scotland we've had the legislation in force for over a year now so we're all quite good at remembering to carry a bag when we go to the shops. And the money saved from the purchase of a plastic bag when you do forget goes towards good causes. Not that we're always forgetting - plastic bag use has dropped by around 80% in the past year.

When I was a child, taking a shopping bag was just what you did. No shopkeeper ever offered a bag for you to use so if you did forget, then it was a case of carrying everything home in your arms. My granny knitted net shopping bags which were light, crunched up small and yet stretched to carry an amazing amount of purchases. In the co-op, butter, cheese and bacon were cut to your requirements and wrapped in greaseproof paper while sugar was scooped out of a sack and weighed into a paper bag which was then double folded to prevent any spillages. Bread came unwrapped and was loaded into the string bag along with the other purchases.

But when we had to buy potatoes then we took the special potato bag with us. This was a battered old brown leather shopper which had seen many years of visits to the co-op and the fruit shop. It had been demoted to potato bag and was regularly loaded with half a stone, or even a stone of loose, unwashed, coated with good Ayrshire soil, potatoes. As a stone was 14lbs (over 6 kilos in today's reckoning) even half a stone of Ayrshires was quite a weight for a skinny kid like me to carry. And add to that, the equally dirty carrots, a piece of turnip and a leek, then no wonder I staggered back home.

When we shopped in a department store for underwear or cotton handkerchiefs, the assistant would wrap your purchase in brown paper. Using a metal rule, she would measure the quantity required from the large roll at the end of the counter, and using the rule as a guide, tear the piece off. Carefully she would place your purchase in the centre and begin the elegant and seemingly complicated task of wrapping it up. Corners were beautifully made and folded over in a perfect triangle, the package turned over to hold them in place, and a huge roll of string produced. A length was skilfully wound round the package first one way and then the other, knotted in the centre and then a loop made from the remainder of the string. This was to make it easy for you to carry with it looped over one finger. Larger purchases such as toys for Christmas were also wrapped in this way though the carrying loop was made of two or three strands of string and much bigger to allow it to slip over the whole hand.

At home, the brown paper and string were carefully removed, folded and put away for further use, like covering school books and jotters.

The sugar bags and even the greaseproof paper from the butter was also saved, the bags for all sorts of uses and the greaseproof paper to grease baking tins and frying pans. Nothing ever went to waste.

We're not quite at that stage of recycling yet, but who knows? Maybe one day, we'll have to be as careful again.

Knit 1, Purl 1, Knit 2 together…

Cast on 48 stitches.....K1P1 rib for 2 inches....continue in stocking stitch until armhole…

We were all familiar with the language of knitting patterns not so long ago as every woman knitted - and quite a few men too! It was the only way to make new things as the shops didn't carry much and what there was, was expensive. If things were really bad and money was tight, then old jumpers would be unravelled, washed and dried to get rid of the wrinkles, and rewound for knitting up into something else.My grandmother was an expert knitter, producing everything from countless jumpers for

Grandma Jane knitted jumpers and socks for us.

my brother and I, to dolls' clothes and swimsuits. But she was renowned for her Argyle patterned socks. These bright socks with their triangles of red, yellow, green and black were knitted on four needles, the different coloured wools being kept separate and tidy on wee holders we named doo-hickeys. Every evening we would hear the click click of these doo-hickeys as she sat at the fire listening to Jimmy Shand and his band on the Scottish Home Service. Her socks were in great demand as Christmas and birthday presents for the menfolk so her needles were always on the go.

Who hasn't experienced the dubious pleasures of a hand-knitted woolly swimsuit? When dry, they gave a certain amount of warmth and covering on a Scottish summer's day at the beach, but venture into the usually freezing water and it was a wonder more of us weren't sucked under by the weight of the swimsuit and drowned as the wool absorbed the sea water. And returning to shore was a struggle with the dead weight of the suit causing it to stretch and sink below our knees. Streaming water, we would struggle up the sand to where our family were sitting wrapped up in coats and scarves,

to receive our chittery bite, usually a bit of chocolate, to stop our teeth chittering from the cold. Those were the days!

Many of us learnt to knit using french knitting. This was a hollow wooden tube with four metal stitch holders on the top. The wool was wound round them and then, using a crochet hook, we passed the wool over each stitch and eventually, out of the bottom of the wooden tube came a coil of knitting. When we had enough we would cast off and wind the woolly coil into a coaster or a mat.

One afternoon a week in primary school was given over to knitting. What the boys did, I have no idea, but we girls sat at our desks and were instructed in the art of knitting, an easy job for the teacher as most of us could already knit. One year we knitted hats, pixie hoods or tammies. I made a tammy in red and beige with a pompom on top and was very pleased with it. A less successful attempt was a pair of socks. They were yellow and I managed the first one quite easily I thought, including turning the heel (a tricky bit) but the teacher pointed out that my tension was too loose and that I should knit the second one more tightly. So I did with the result that the second one did look a lot neater and less bed-sock like than the first one, but was also a good bit smaller than it. But they made good dusters with your hand inside them!

Grandma Jane knitted everything for me.

The prospect of a new baby had everyone get out their knitting needles and white baby wool and set to creating everything a baby would need; a shawl of course, often knitted on fine needles with 2ply wool. It was as light as gossamer and often intricately patterned, but warm and cosy and soft for a newborn. Then there were cardigans and coats and leggings and bonnets and vests and bootees and mittens as well to complete the layette. A new mum with a family of knitters to rely on was never short of baby clothes. As the baby grew, the knitters would supply dresses and jumpers and romper suits using blue wool for a boy and pink for a girl. Sometimes they would use a pale green or a lemon. I knitted my first-born an outfit comprising jumper, cardigan and leggings in red and white and felt myself very trendy.

All my own work!

I famously knitted myself a mini-dress in a sludge green which was very useful as it never crushed as well as being warm (for the parts it covered) with its long sleeves and polo neck. It lasted for years or at least until miniskirts were overtaken by midis.

Most of my dress was knitted in my lunch hour at the school where I taught. We had separate male and female staff-rooms where no doubt, the men discussed football in theirs, whereas in ours, we all knitted. Nowadays such behaviour would be frowned on.

One of my friends in another school confessed that when she had the children all working quietly, she would take out her knitting and do a few rows. What would the inspectors have made of it if she'd been spotted?

For skilled knitters there were more complex patterns to try like Aran with its cables and twists and Fair Isle knitting with the colourful patterns. When I lived in Canada, my friend Margaret did a roaring trade in Aran jumpers as her mum back in Scotland was an expert knitter and could churn them out. The wool was much cheaper than in Canada so Margaret took orders for her mum who posted the finished article to her for passing on to her customer. Her mum was able to fly to Canada on the proceeds!

Before the advent of cheap knitted goods and knitting machines, everything had to be knitted; tea cosies, hot water bottle covers, bed jackets, body warmers, bathroom mats, cushions and bedspreads as well as many other items. And let's not forget crochet; anything that could be knitted could also be crocheted. Who could forget the milk jug cover with the beads along the edge? There was even a crochet pattern for a bra though I doubt it would give much support to anyone over a 32 inch bust. Crochet could produce intricate patterns especially popular for dressing table sets and doilies, and very fine work like lace edgings.

Knitting is experiencing a revival though, for some ardent knitters, it has never gone away. But now the cost of balls of wool has increased greatly and can't compete with the knits on sale in the shops. They're usually made on machines in the poorer parts of the world and as such, are sold very cheaply.

Knitting is a very relaxing hobby to have and keeps the fingers flexible and busy when there's nothing much on the TV and stops me delving into the biscuit box. A friend of mine was wearing, one very cold day, a cosy thick jumper in an Icelandic pattern which she'd knitted herself and was of a far superior quality to anything she could buy. And it was also quite beautiful. Maybe I'll try that next.

Overland to Switzerland!

I was going Abroad! Out of this country and into another, away from familiarity, Abroad! I'd always wanted to go and when I discovered that my school ran trips Abroad for pupils in 4th year, I couldn't wait to reach that milestone. I spent my 3rd year when I turned 15 at a Saturday job earning a little money to help with the cost of the following year's trip.

And when I heard that that year's trip was to Switzerland I was elated. Not your ordinary school trip to France or Belgium but Switzerland, land of mountains and cuckoo clocks, yodelling and army knives.

...and alpenhorns!

Five of us from my school joined up with two other schools for the trip. We were all girls from Queen's Park Senior Secondary, joining up with Hillhead and Hyndland. My two best friends, Barbara and Annette were going too, so after our O grades were finished in June, we set off by train, wearing our school uniforms of course, on the long journey to Brunnen on Lake Lucerne.

It took two days and nights sitting up in packed compartments, on wooden seats at one point so we must have been pretty tired and whiffy when we eventually arrived. We didn't care. We were Abroad! And not only that, we were staying in what was the height of luxury to us, the Hotel Eden, almost on the lakeshore.

Even better was to come. The teachers (none of whom were from our school and who all seemed to our eyes incredibly young compared to the ones we were used to)

Going up!

simply told us to do whatever we wanted while they got on with their activities. At one point we spotted them on a seesaw in a children's playpark, giggling as they swung up and down. None of us could imagine our teachers doing that.

But the highlight was when we discovered that a posse of Hillhead boys were on the trip. Never mind the stunning scenery, the paddle boats criss-crossing Lake Lucerne, the man playing his alpenhorn, what was all that compared with a group of equally star-struck young lads?

Me and chalet!

So we set off to explore the town (and pursue the boys) and try out our German on the long-suffering shop assistants. Barbara was keen to buy her Dad a pipe-rack so she rehearsed what she would say before she went in to what she thought was a tobacconist's. The man shook his head and said something so Barbara repeated her spiel. At this the man gesticulated somewhat exuberantly and eventually we worked out that we weren't actually in the tobacconist's, this was the pharmacy next door.

There were a couple of trips organised for us; a trip to the top of Mount Pilatus by chairlift and cable car, a new experience for all of us. It was pretty chilly at the top but luckily we'd all brought our school blazers to wear! And then a visit to Schwyz, which is known as the home of Swiss army knives and the founding of Switzerland.

I bought several souvenirs, in particular a Swiss musical box in the shape of a chalet which tinkled away for many years before gently expiring. I couldn't afford a cuckoo clock, they were just out of reach of my spending money.

It was a memorable trip and for me it was the start of my itchy feet and wanderings around the world. I contacted Barbara and Annette again for their memories of this trip and we met up to laugh over our young selves and our first trip Abroad.

Work Experience - Old Style

The moment I turned 15, I got a Saturday job in the new Littlewoods store in the centre of Glasgow. My job was down in the basement where the fruit and vegetables were prepared before being taken up to the shop. I spent the whole day, chopping off the ends of cabbages and cauliflowers, unwrapping individual tomatoes (yes, they each came wrapped in tissue paper) and making up bunches of parsley before trundling the lot into the lift and filling up the counters in the shop. For all that hard work, I received 14/9d.

I wasn't a great success at it as I got into trouble for piling up bunches of grapes on top of each other. After all, they were a luxury fruit! However I stuck at it and saved as much as I could out of my wages until, after nine long months, I had enough to buy a transistor radio to listen to Radio Luxembourg. Then I handed in my notice.

Betty worked on Saturdays in her local Woolworths for 10/6d and was given a filthy overall to wear. So dirty was it, her mother made her leave it at the front door when she came home for lunch. And when she saw one of her relatives come into the store, she ducked down below the counter so they wouldn't see her!

Jane went for a Saturday job in what was described as a turf accountant's as she was good at maths and thought she'd enjoy it. Imagine her surprise when she discovered it was a bookie's! However she did get a job in a tartan gift shop and was thrilled to meet Johnny Cash when he came in to buy some souvenirs before returning to the US.

Some jobs were pretty awful. Mike worked in a stick factory, using electric saws to cut up railway sleepers and then putting them into the splitting machine. He then bundled the sticks up with wire and filled the centres with shavings before dipping them in naphthalene to make firelighters. He had no gloves or protective clothing so his hands were red and raw after every Saturday there. Health and safety were entirely non-existent then.

Other jobs were considered quite posh. Meg was a waitress in a tea-room which boasted white linen tablecloths and cake stands. Unfortunately it was quite near a football ground and one Saturday, a well-refreshed gent came in after the match and ordered a coffee. When it came, he shook the pepper-pot liberally over it, stirred it in, took a sip, and announced it wasn't Bovril! It certainly wasn't but he took some convincing that he'd actually ordered coffee.

In between times, we babysat, did hotel work, laboured on building sites and temped in offices but when we were older and studying at college and university, it was essential to work over the long summer vacation to fund the next year's study. We could be more adventurous and travel further afield.

One year I worked as a barmaid at a holiday camp in Somerset. The bar I worked in was in the bingo hall. While games were in progress, we had no customers but once someone called 'House!' the stampede began. Hordes of men descended, all shouting complicated orders at us which had to be filled before the next game started. And all the while, adding up the total cost in pounds, shillings and pence in our heads as we weren't

I'm in the middle.

allowed to write it down. No doubt some customers got bargains while others must have thought the drinks expensive.

David worked in a frozen pea factory in Norfolk where he spent the summer months sweeping up the peas that landed on the floor. Boring, repetitive but quite well paid, although he's never been too keen on frozen peas since.

Uncertificated teaching was popular but was only possible in June and September as the schools were on holiday the rest of the summer. It was, however, reasonably well-paid compared to other jobs, though letting students with no training whatsoever loose in a classroom of teenagers could have interesting results. At least it let us find out if teaching was for us before embarking on teacher training college.

I was an auxiliary nurse in a psychiatric hospital in Sussex one year. I loved the job, which was mainly working with elderly patients who not only had mental problems but were also physically ill. We had to wear the full nurse's uniform complete with stiff, starched collars, belts and cuffs and finished off with a jaunty white cap. For going out, we even had long thick capes lined in red. Matron was the typical termagant of the time and told me to take out my gold sleeper ear-rings when on duty! There was a large

group of students working at the hospital and staying in the nurses' home, so there was lots of fun to be had when off duty.

I also worked as an auxiliary nurse in a hospital for mentally handicapped people in Edinburgh, and again lived in the Nurses' Home which was situated in the wooded grounds of the hospital. The Nurses' Home unfortunately was targeted by a certain type of male who relished making obscene calls to it, and we had to deal with quite a few. One night, a particularly nasty caller threatened to come to the Home so we contacted the duty matron and asked if we should call the police.

'Not at all,' was the reply and she duly got on her bicycle and cycled through the dark woods looking for the perpetrator. Goodness knows what she'd have done with him if she'd found him.

Christmas meant working in the Post Office, either in the sorting office or out delivering the huge sacks of Christmas mail round the Glasgow streets. It was a toss up which was better; the warmth of the sorting office albeit with the boss glaring down at you, or the often cold, wet outdoors but with no-one keeping an eye on you as you wandered about, so that a bit of Christmas shopping was possible, though strictly forbidden. Sandra met her boss when she was in Lewis's department store in Argyle St with her delivery bag still bulging, but as he shouldn't have been there either, nothing was said.

Working in the Post Office didn't stop us enjoying the round of parties and nights out. I remember teetering home in the early hours from a dinner dance, changing out of my party clothes and heading out again to catch the first bus of the morning up to the sorting office, my long hair still in its coils and curls on top of my head. I did my full shift but I couldn't guarantee the accuracy of my sorting that day.

It was all great experience and we learned a lot both about work and ourselves, plus it gave us the motivation and the finances to carry on our studies for another year or so.

I'm on the right.

Are ye dancin?

Are ye dancin'?
Naw, it's just the funny way ah'm staunin'.
The classic Glasgow response to a request for a dance!

I first started going to the dancing on a Saturday night when I was fifteen and in 4th year at school. The girl I sat beside in French went to Netherlee Scout Hall, on the south side of the city, where dances were held every week, so I tagged along with her.

This was in the days of Trad Jazz, the Clyde Valley Stompers and the George Penman Band and it was guaranteed to set your feet tapping. Dancing was dancing in those days; the boy put his arm around you in the classic ballroom way and you birled around the dance floor in a one, two, three, shuffle move. One of the most popular tunes was Wimoweh which was picked up by Kenny Ball and his Jazzmen and recorded by the Tokens as The Lion Sleeps Tonight.

The other popular dance in our area was at Whitecraigs Tennis Club but it was considered a bit posh, frequented as it was by boys from Allan Glen's and Hutchie, fee-paying schools in Glasgow.

I was once taken to the Flamingo (or the Flamin' O as it was popularly known) in Cardonald, in the south-west of Glasgow, by my cousin who was convinced it was time I saw the bright lights. It was certainly a very modern, large dance hall but I didn't fancy it much. I never went again.

As I got older, bolder and the music changed to rock and pop, I ventured into Glasgow to the Cave under the railway arches in Midland Street. It prided itself on being Glasgow's answer to the Cavern and no doubt it was as dark and smoky as the original Liverpool one.

It was there one night that I heard of the assassination of President Kennedy, while dancing with my then boyfriend. The news certainly changed the atmosphere in the club.

Another Glasgow venue I discovered was the Maryland off Sauchiehall Street. I had been attending ballroom dancing classes at Roger McEwan's School of Dance on Scott Street, why I don't know as we only did the Shake and the Twist at the dancing. But cha cha cha I did and decided to try the Saturday nights there. It was an odd place with two rooms between which was the stage. In one room, the band faced you, and in the other, the room you went to when you got a lumber (the Glasgow term for 'clicking' with a boy), you got the band's back view. Not that that mattered as your attention was focussed on the lad dancing with you. The dim lighting helped soften the features of the plooky young man you'd landed with.

The Plaza ballroom at Eglinton Toll was quite close to where I lived but you only went there for special occasions. It had a fountain in the middle of the dance floor and chairs and tables on a raised platform around the sides. One unfortunate young lady I remember shifted her seat too close to the edge and tumbled backwards on to the dance floor. I went to a 21st held at the Plaza where we had dinner first followed by a dance. I wore a two piece green satin outfit which I had made myself and had white satin shoes dyed green to match. My long hair was up in a bouffant and sprayed solid and I felt very sophisticated being there.

Getting ready for the dancing.

I only went to the Barrowland once where my partner was flummoxed by the band announcing the twist, which he patently could not do so we never went there again. It was also quite a distance away, as was the Dennistoun Palais. The Locarno was also considered out of bounds, frequented as it was by the American sailors from the HolyLoch, though I did meet my eventual husband there at a student Beatnik Ball during Charities Week.

The student union dances became available (you couldn't get in unless you could show your Matric card) when I attended Glasgow University. The Queen Margaret Union (the women's union) was favoured over the Men's Union, as the dances there never started until the bar closed by which time the male students were far too drunk to dance. Strathclyde University dances were popular due to the number of Norwegian students and the possibility of bumping into Bobby McGregor, the Scottish swimming champion who was studying architecture at the Uni.

But my dancing days came to an end when I left University, got married and became a teacher. However, let me hear anything played by the likes of theTemperance Seven and my feet are sure to start tapping again.

Frills, Fur and Flowers

I was very pleased when minis became the fashion in the late 1960's as being tall, I had trouble getting anything that didn't creep above my knees. But money was tight so each purchase was carefully considered before buying. One of my best buys was an off-white wool dress with black braid which was on sale and which was supposed to fit a large-size petite woman. But it fitted me so I bought it and it saw many outings over the years.

Likewise an orange polyester dress from C&A which didn't crush, didn't need ironing and washed and dried in a flash. Perfect!

Then we moved to Toronto where everything changed, including me. We both had jobs, there was some money to spare and there was a wee dress shop on the block close to our apartment. Out went my carefully considered approach to buying clothes, and in came visits to the dress shop where the owner was only too keen to encourage my profligacy.

I bought some pretty disastrous outfits on the spur of the moment but wore them regardless, as after all, I had spent good money on them. There was a floaty blue-green creation made of chiffon type material (mini of course) with long floaty sleeves which kept getting caught on door handles and dipping into pasta sauces.

Another was a bright pink mini caught under the bust à la Jane Austen, again with long wide sleeves but this time with pink fur round them. Baby doll is the term that comes to mind. Gruesome but again, it was worn to various parties and get-togethers.

The worst one of the lot was an all-in-one Spanish type outfit which consisted of wide knee-length trousers, a frilly white blouse and a black waistcoat. This was worn with black patent boots. It had two main problems; it was all-in-one and, as I said, I'm tall so it was just that little bit too short in the body for me. It made me want to stoop all the time. Standing up straight was well nigh impossible.

Not my favourite!

The other problem was going to the toilet. It had to be pre-planned as it took a lot of time. The zip ran down the back of the outfit so I had to manoeuvre myself to unzip it, then step out of the whole thing, while balancing precariously on the afore-mentioned high-heeled black patent boots. Afterwards, the whole process was gone through in reverse. I remember passing it on to a second-hand clothes store where it hung in the window unsold for ages.

But my most favourite outfit was a long cream dress with brown daisies sewn around the waist and high neck. I loved it and it did me good service for quite a while. I went blonde and grew my hair longer so I looked a right swell when I wore it. At least, I thought I did. It made up for all the other disastrous outfits I'd bought.

My buying spree only lasted two years as we then moved to a small rural town in Australia where the nearest fashionable dress shop was 250 miles away. And anyway, there weren't many opportunities for dressing up there, shorts, t-shirts and flip-flops being the order of the day.

Definitely my favourite!